Seven Days with the

Gospel of Mark

For a Personal or Shared Retreat

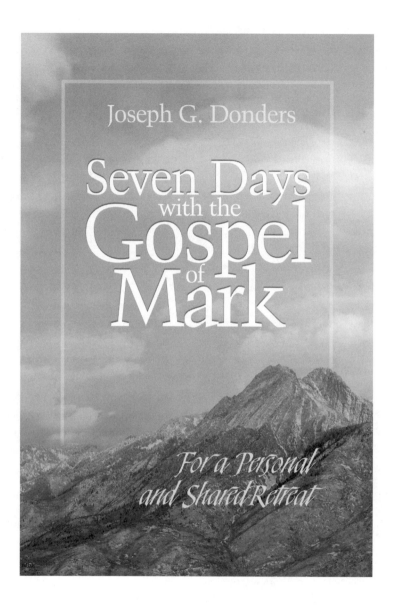

Joseph G. Donders

Seven Days
with the
Gospel
of
Mark

*For a Personal
and Shared Retreat*

TWENTY-THIRD PUBLICATIONS

185 WILLOW STREET • PO BOX 180 • MYSTIC, CT 06355
TEL: 1-800-321-0411 • FAX: 1-800-572-0788
E-MAIL: ttpubs@aol.com • www.twentythirdpublications.com

Twenty-Third Publications
A Division of Bayard
185 Willow Street
P.O. Box 180
Mystic, CT 06355
(860) 536-2611
(800) 321-0411
www.twentythirdpublications.com

ISBN:1-58595-319-9
Library of Congress Catalog Card Number: 2003113259
Printed in the U.S.A.

CONTENTS

SUGGESTIONS FOR MAKING A RETREAT

Prepare a quiet place where you can make your retreat. Set up a few symbols that might help create a prayerful atmosphere, such as a statue, a cross, an icon, or a candle. Sit in a comfortable chair. Have a notebook ready to write down your thoughts, feelings, and ideas.

Set a time limit for your reflection; a half-hour to an hour per meditation might do. Use the morning meditation before you begin your day, and the evening meditation either at the end of your work day or before going to bed.

Avoid distractions; try to relax and empty your mind of all worries and concerns. Know that you are in God's presence, that God is present in you, your family, your community, and the world.

Read the Scripture passage cited at the beginning of each meditation. Allow the words to fill your mind. Pause at the words or phrases that speak to you in a particular way, that touch your mind or your heart. Reflect on how the Scripture texts relate to you, your work, your relationships, and your life. The suggestions in the *For Reflection* section will help spark some ideas.

Try to listen to what the Spirit is saying to you. Remember that the most important part of prayer is to be attentive to God's word. Be open to that word, even when it challenges you to live as you have never lived before.

Pray for all those who are making a retreat at the same time as you, and who might even be using this same book. Ask that all of you may be blessed with the knowledge that the Spirit of God is always present, always calling us forward.

Begin a journal that you will use throughout the retreat. Record in it your thoughts and prayers, as well as the moments when you are most aware of God's presence in your life. (There are pages for journaling in the back of this book, starting on p. 51.)

INTRODUCTION

The gospel of Mark is an excellent companion for prayer and reflection. It is a treasure chest full of insights and surprises, and therefore, a wonderful retreat guide.

Through the pages of this little book, I invite you to reflect on Mark's gospel and use it to make a mini-retreat, a prayerful time away in the midst of your daily tasks and responsibilities. This may mean getting up earlier than usual for a morning meditation, and putting aside tasks earlier than usual for an evening meditation. During this seven-day period we will focus together on the spiritual advice found in the gospel of Mark. We will follow the developments—the ups and downs—in the discoveries made by the people who surrounded Jesus.

Every book has its own dynamics. Few people would take a book, read one chapter or a few paragraphs from it, then feel they had the whole story. Yet when reading sacred Scripture—including the gospels—we usually read just small fragments: a snippet here and a snippet there. It is not often, for example, that we read a whole gospel from beginning to end. The result is that the inherent meaning and purpose of each book of the Bible can be overlooked.

This is certainly true of the four gospels. Each gospel has its own approach and its own message. Each introduces Jesus in its own way, and is written in response to different needs and different times. Each of the four evangelists tells their story with the desire to help us relate the story to our own lives.

Mark's gospel reads like a mystery. He wants us to decipher this mystery, to resolve a secret. Who is this Jesus the gospel writes about, and what are his intentions? Why doesn't anyone seem to understand him? How should we relate to him? Why does his gospel start with the words, "The beginning of the good news of Jesus Christ, the Son of God"? What is that good news? What does its beginning mean to me? Is there going to be bad news as well? Where do I enter the story? *Do* I enter the story?

1

Mark himself remains a bit of a mystery. Most commentators think that he never had any actual contact with Jesus, though some traditions identify him as the young man who runs away naked at the arrest of Jesus (Mk 14:51). Papias, a bishop who lived around 160 CE, mentions that Mark was Peter's interpreter, and that his book reflects Peter's teaching and the faith of Peter's community in Rome. According to others there might even have been a blood relation between Peter and Mark, as in his first letter Peter mentions "my son Mark" (5:13).

Mark, who devised the gospel form and is generally considered the first gospel author, tells a straightforward story. His gospel is the shortest of the four, comprised of sixteen chapters and six hundred and seventy-seven verses. You can read it in about one and a half hours. (It might be good to read through the whole of Mark's gospel before you start this retreat.)

Seven Days with the Gospel of Mark offers suggestions for a morning and evening meditation. The length of that prayerful reflection can differ from person to person and from community to community, but the ideal would be to spend from half an hour to an hour on each session. You can meditate in the quiet of your room, in a church, or even outside—anywhere you feel prayerfully at home with yourself and God's Spirit. There are also suggested questions for your reflection, to help you consider how Mark's gospel applies to your everyday life, as well as a morning and evening prayer you can use to end your meditation. Finally, there is a faith response for each of the seven days.

You can make this retreat alone, with a friend, or with several other people. It can also be adapted to seven weeks, or whatever time period suits your needs.

As we make our retreat, we will reflect on some of the main points in the gospel of Mark. In doing so, we pray that the words of Jesus may affect our lives today as they did the lives of those he touched long ago.

May we come to a new understanding not only of the life of Jesus, but of our own lives, too.

FIRST DAY

The beginning of the good news
of Jesus Christ, the Son of God.

Read Mark 1:1–13

In most translations of Scripture, Mark's book is called *The Gospel According to Mark*. Most likely, what we read now as the first line of his gospel was meant to be read as the title to the book: "The Beginning of the Good News of Jesus Christ, the Son of God."

Mark wrote these words to describe something completely new in this world, a newness people had been waiting for every time they encountered selfishness and misery. Would there be no light to break through their darkness? Would goodness ever overcome the bad in the world? Would there ever be a "new beginning," a new order to life? These people waited in hope that there would be an end to all evil.

The most recent prophetic voice expressing the certainty of that hope had been heard in the Book of Malachi, written some three hundred years before Mark wrote his gospel. Malachi was the last of the minor prophets, so called because of the brevity of their books and of their message. He writes:

> See I am sending my messenger to prepare the way before me, and the Lord whom you seek will suddenly come to his temple (Mal 3:1).

Malachi also indicated the radical change this messenger would bring when he described how he would be like a refiner's fire that would change and refine the world (Mal 3:2b–3). But in the three hundred years since Malachi's prophecy there had been a deafening silence. No word had been heard, no sign had been seen. The waiting had produced a great and growing anxiety.

Mark begins his gospel telling us how, as suddenly as a flash of lightning in a pitch dark night, John appears at the river Jordan. He is dressed like Elijah and the prophets of old, wearing camel's hair with a leather belt, and he is eating the produce of the desert. To explain his appearance Mark quotes the prophecy of Malachi cited here. He does not mention Malachi's name but that of another prophet, Isaiah, in describing John the Baptizer's mission as the voice of one crying out in the wilderness, preparing the way of the Lord.

John baptizes with water and announces the one who will be more powerful than he himself, one who will baptize with the Holy Spirit. People come from all over to listen to him. They line up in front of him, confessing their sins and hoping for a change in their lives and in the world, and John baptizes them.

Lining up with those who are hoping for change is Jesus of Nazareth. John baptizes him as well, and as Jesus comes up out of the water the heavens open, God's Spirit descends on him, and a voice is heard: "You are my Son, the Beloved; with you I am well pleased" (1:11). Here the story takes another turn as God's Spirit drives Jesus—"immediately" the text insists—into the wilderness. (We find the word "immediately" being used some twenty-seven times in Mark's gospel!) Jesus remains in the desert for forty days. This number echoes the forty years that the Hebrew people wandered in the desert after the exodus from Egypt, before reaching the Promised Land.

In the desert, Jesus is confronted and tempted by Satan. He struggles with the "wild beasts," metaphors for the evil that terrorizes this world. Mark further tells us that angels sustained Jesus during those forty days, reminding us of the manna sent to the Israelites during their time in the desert.

You may be able to identify with Jesus' desert experience as you begin this retreat. You might see yourself in the people who came from all over Judea and Jerusalem to hear John the Baptizer preach, people who were spiritually hungry, waiting to be fed. They came because they were looking for a change, a transformation both of themselves and of the world. Jesus joined them in the river Jordan to show his compassion and empathy, and to help them find what they were looking for.

Before you continue on this retreat, ask yourself: would you really go and listen to a prophet like John, who preached repentance and a radical change for the world? More than that, would you really be willing to listen to his words and enact a radical change in your life? Are you willing to be found in the company of Jesus, who will bring about that change?

We cannot be like sick people who do not want to go to a doctor because they are afraid to hear that they may have to change their lives. Be ready and willing to plunge into the saving waters of baptism. Let the good news of Jesus Christ, the Son of God, bring you the change you long for in your life.

FOR REFLECTION

- Why are you making this retreat?

- Are you willing to stand with the people who came to hear John?

- Spend some time reflecting on how your own baptism mirrors the baptism of Jesus in the river Jordan.

- The Holy Spirit moves Jesus to tackle the evil in this world. How do you follow his example in your own life?

MORNING PRAYER

Almighty Father, the coming of your Son among us
is a divine sign of the hope you invest in us.
Let me catch something of that hope in my daily life. Amen.

FAITH RESPONSE FOR TODAY

Read a newspaper, watch a TV newscast or listen to one on the radio today. Reflecting on what you have read or heard, who do you think would be most interested in Mark's good news today?

EVENING   MEDITATION

"The time is fulfilled...follow me."

Read Mark 1:14–20

When John the Baptizer is arrested, Jesus assumes his ministry as prophesied in Isaiah. He leaves Judea, with its temple and ruling classes, and goes to the region of Galilee. Once there, he sums up his mission in about twenty words: "The time is fulfilled, and the kingdom of God has come near; repent and believe in the good news" (1:15).

Jesus uses the Greek word *kairos* for "time." This word defines time not by reading a clock or noting the date on a calendar, but as a decisive moment, now or never. It indicates an opportunity, a challenge. One has to choose, because the kingdom of God is near. The great change hoped for by the people who crowded around John the Baptizer is going to be fulfilled.

Another word found in Mark 1:15 is "kingdom." This word was filled with meaning in Jesus' days, but it is a term that can be misunderstood in our democratic way of life. Jesus uses the word as a metaphor for the rule of God existing in people's hearts. It means to share in God's attitude toward ourselves, others, the world, and the universe. Recent popes have used the phrase "the civilization of love" to describe this state.

The arrival of this new order, the kingdom of God, implies the beginning of a change in our world. The old regime is over; a new one is coming in. It is the beginning of a drama in which the world as we know it—the present age, as some would call it—has reached its end. It is a question of a process: growing out of the old into the new. The challenge made to all of us, to take up the course of action indicated by Jesus' words: "repent and believe in the good news".

The Greek word *metanoia*, which is used for the word "repent," does not mean to don sackcloth and ashes, and do penance. It even means more than changing one's mind. *Metanoia* involves a total reorientation of one's personality, a turn around, a conversion. One's whole attitude has to change. This change is further clarified with the phrase "and believe in the good news."

The word "believe" must be understood within this context, as well. Here it is not only a kind of intellectual assent, as in "I believe this," or "I believe that." Here the word refers to an attitude in life that influences all we decide to do or not do, all we choose to be or not be.

A simple example might illustrate this point. You have a friend who has a very precious and costly string of pearls. She is going on a holiday and does not want to take them with her, nor does she want to leave them at home. So she comes to ask you whether you can keep them for her during her absence. You agree to hold the pearls for your friend, and she gives them to you in a closed and sealed parcel, which you carefully hide in a safe place in your house. Yet the presence of this box with its precious contents is going to influence your behavior up to the moment your friend returns.

Continuing on in the first chapter of Mark, we find the first thing Jesus does as he begins his public ministry is to engaging others in his mission. Passing along the Sea of Galilee (in fact it is only a lake) he sees some fishermen, Simon and his brother Andrew. He asks them to follow him, and they "immediately" do so (1:17–18). The same happens in the next two verses, with James and his brother John.

Having "fished" these four men out of the world in which they lived, inviting them to enter the new order he brought from his Father, Jesus tells them: "Follow me and I will make you fish for people." He asks them to be his disciples and to share in his mission, helping him to bring others out of the present age and into the new world of God's kingdom.

These four men do not choose Jesus; it is he who calls them. Likewise, it is he who is calling us. Our belief in the arrival of God's kingdom in our world should be the determining factor in our lives, as it became the determining factor in the lives of his first disciples.

There is a different interpretation of why the first disciples were called "fishermen." This is a term sometimes used in Hebrew Scripture for those sent by Yahweh to "fish" the unjust and their injustices out of the world. The prophet Jeremiah wrote:

I am now sending for many fishermen, says the Lord, and they shall catch them....For my eyes are on all their ways; they are not hidden from my presence, nor is their iniquity concealed from my sight (16:16–17).

And centuries later the prophet Amos would prophesy:

Hear this word, you...who oppress the poor, who crush the needy.... The Lord has sworn by his holiness: the time is surely coming upon you, when they shall take you away with hooks, even the last one of you with fishhooks (4:1–2).

It does not much matter which interpretation we choose of why Jesus' first disciples were called "fishermen." In either case the mission given to them and to us is the same; to "fish for people."

Jesus came to change this world. He came to introduce what in Hebrew tradition is often called *tikkun olam*, the restoration of the world. This restoration asks for the twofold response as indicated by Jesus' words, "Repent and believe in the good news." It is a challenge made to us not only as individuals but also as members of the world in which we live.

How will we respond? What will our response entail? Where will it lead us?

FOR REFLECTION

• How do you react to Jesus' invitation to be his disciple?

• What does the introduction of God's rule in this world mean to you on a personal level?

• Is there anyone among your friends or acquaintances whom you would describe as someone who tries to live by the standards of the kingdom of God? How do they do this?

EVENING PRAYER

Our Father, who art in heaven, hallowed be thy name.
Thy kingdom come, thy will be done on earth as it is in heaven.

SECOND DAY

"A new teaching—with authority!"

Read Mark 1:21-39

Jesus has called his first four disciples, and now they go to Capernaum. It is an interesting choice, as it will become the place where Jesus makes his home. A small harbor town in Galilee, Capernaum was one of the more cosmopolitan cities in that region. Its population consisted of many different ethnic groups.

Jesus and his disciples wait until the Sabbath day to go to the synagogue, where Jesus starts to teach. In Mark's gospel, Jesus does not talk much; there are no long discourses as there are in the other gospels. Mark's gospel is filled more with deeds and less with words. Yet that morning Jesus begins his public ministry by teaching.

Mark does not explain what Jesus taught that day. We can, however, guess his topic. Most likely, he was speaking to the people gathered in the temple about the introduction of God's kingdom, of the rule of God: "The kingdom of God has come near; repent, and believe in the good news."

Mark is more interested in telling us the reaction of the people to Jesus. His listeners are amazed by the way he teaches, and by the effect that teaching has on them. They were astounded by his personal authority, his positive certainty. His message was like a breath of fresh air. Jesus told them what they had been hoping for so long to hear. Listening to him they discovered their own potential. Listening to him they discovered their own deepest desires, their own true identity, their existence as beings filled with God's breath.

9

A musical example might help to illustrate what happened to the people that day. Picture a grand piano standing in a spacious and open room. The lid is open, and the hammers and strings of the piano are visible. You stand some distance from the piano with a tuning fork. You hit the tuning fork on the wood of a table, and the vibration of the tone fills the whole room. You put your hand on the tuning fork to silence it. And—if all goes well!—the string of the grand piano that corresponds to the tone of your tuning fork has picked up its vibration and is singing on its own.

Something like that happened that afternoon at the temple in Capernaum. Jesus touched something in the people there. They were on his wavelength; they resonated with his promising words.

Then a man whose life had become like a nightmare because he was possessed by an evil spirit began to shout: "What have you to do with us, Jesus of Nazareth? Have you come to destroy us? I know who you are, the Holy One of God" (1:24). Now we read the first words Jesus spoke that day in Capernaum. He says to the evil possessing the man, "Be silent, and come out of him." After some convulsions, that is exactly what happens. The onlookers are amazed, asking themselves and each other: "What is this? A new teaching—with authority! He commands even the unclean spirits, and they obey him" (1:27).

We know what this is, as do all those who read Mark's gospel, because he had informed them from the first line of his gospel: Jesus Christ, the Son of God. But the people in Capernaum did not know. They had no answer to their questions, though after hearing Jesus teach and after witnessing this exorcism they helped spread Jesus' fame throughout the land. The newness of the good news of God's reign had begun to invade the old state of affairs, starting on the holy ground of the temple, a place ruled and organized by the theologians, liturgists, and scribes of the day.

After the events in the temple, Simon invites Jesus home for the Sabbath meal. Simon, later on called Peter by Jesus, must have been married because his mother-in-law was at the house, in bed with a fever. They told Jesus about it and without any further ado he went to her bed, took her by the hand, and healed her. She, in turn, began to prepare a meal for them.

Here we see that Jesus would perform his work not only in an astounding manner, as in the temple that day, but also in the ordinary events of everyday life. Thus we know that the kingdom of God, our sharing in God's love, is with us every minute of the day and night, in the most ordinary things of life. It is here that we weave our lives together with God.

It is evening and the Sabbath rest is over. By now the word about Jesus has spread. People from all over who are sick or traumatized in one way or another are being brought to him. It is as if Jesus' example of care and concern revitalized this instinct in others, so that they bring to him those in need of help. And Jesus responds by healing, laying on hands, and casting out evil spirits.

Night falls. People go home, and Jesus and his companions go to sleep. Early the next morning, while it is still dark, Jesus awakes, goes to a quiet place outside, and prays. But as soon as it grows light those who had not been able to be touched by Jesus the day before start again to gather at Simon's home.

Simon and the three others hunt for Jesus, and when they find him, they ask him to come back to Simon's house: "Everyone is searching for you." He refuses to come. It is the first disagreement between Jesus and the disciples. Jesus refuses to restrict himself to the circle they want to draw around him. It is a temptation that will confront so many of his followers down through the centuries, as they call on Jesus to serve them and their needs exclusively.

Jesus tells them that he is called to others, too: "Let us go on to the neighboring towns, so that I may proclaim the message there also; for that is what I came out to do" (1:38). Jesus came to bring all of us together. Are we ready to join with him in this mission?

FOR REFLECTION

- What is your favorite gospel story? Why is it your favorite?

- Do you relate your daily tasks to what Jesus called the arrival of the kingdom of God? How do you understand the kingdom as present in your everyday life?

- Jesus refuses to be exclusive in his mission. What can you do to open the circle of your own Christian outreach?

MORNING PRAYER

*Dear Jesus, you call us to be engaged in bringing about
your Father's kingdom. Help me to do so with open arms
and an open heart, welcoming all. Amen.*

FAITH RESPONSE FOR TODAY

When you need to make a decision today, do so with the intention of
fostering the interests of God's kingdom, the civilization of love.

EVENING MEDITATION

"Your sins are forgiven."

Read Mark 1:40—2:17

In our reading this morning we found out that Jesus had left those who were waiting to be healed in Capernaum, telling his disciples that he must proclaim the arrival of God's kingdom to other places as well. But there was also another reason that he wanted to move on.

Jesus did not object to healings; indeed he would perform them up to his last days in Mark's gospel. He had come to heal the world, to restore God's rule, but that involved more than physically healing the sick and the obsessed. Jesus had come to heal the world at a deeper level, to heal the minds and hearts and souls of those in need. That is why he tells the leper after he is healed, "See that you say nothing to anyone" (1:44).

You might compare this with the experience of a group of Medical Mission Sisters who went to work in an underdeveloped country. They built a clinic, the first one in the region. People came from all over to be healed. After some time the sisters discovered that the same patients were coming again and again to the clinic with the same diseases, mainly intestinal. So the sisters went out to the hamlets where their patients lived, and found that the water there was in an unhealthy condition. In response, they organized a program to educate the people about clean water, and in no time the number of patients who needed treatment diminished. The cause of the disease had been discovered and dealt with.

The experience of the sisters might help us understand the case of the paralyzed man, which is the next healing Jesus performs. This story begins with an interesting detail; the paralytic is brought in by four men. We also learn that Jesus is touched by the behavior of these four men, who went out of their way to have their friend healed. In their actions, he must have recognized his Father, source of all benevolent goodness and in whose image we are all created.

The crowd made it impossible to get the stretcher through the door of the house, which may have been the house in which Jesus lived during his time in Capernaum. So the four went literally "over the top" in their compassion, and lowered the man down through the roof of the house, right in front of Jesus. Touched by their kindness and faith, Jesus tells the man on his stretcher: "Son, your sins are forgiven" (2:5).

Here Jesus touches that which underlies all the ills of this world: he heals the man of his sin before he cures his disability. Sin is the root cause of all that needs healing not because our ills are a punishment for sinfulness, but because they are so often—maybe always—its effect.

There were some scribes present in that overcrowded house. Though they kept silent, Jesus knew what they were thinking. How can a human being forgive sins? Only God can do that, only God can heal and restore in that way. That is why Jesus says to them:

> "Why do you raise such questions in your hearts? Which is easier, to say to the paralytic, 'Your sins are forgiven,' or to say, 'Stand up and take up your mat and walk'?" (2:8-9).

Jesus then turned to the lame man on the stretcher and told him to stand up, take his mat, and go home. And again using the word that he favors, "immediately," Mark tells us that this was what the man did as those around him comment: "We have never seen anything like this." The man was healed both physically and spiritually.

The story that follows is about a tax collector, someone who, in those days, was considered something of a sinner and a collaborator in the oppression of the poor. As Jesus is walking along the lake he sees Levi, the son of Alphaeus, sitting at his tax booth. He invites him: "Follow me."

Before Levi does that he throws a farewell party for his fellow tax collectors and other doubtful characters. Jesus and his disciples are invited as well. Some of the scribes see this, and they complain not to Jesus, but to some of his disciples, asking, "Why does he eat with tax collectors and sinners?" The disciples, in turn, tell Jesus, who replies:

> "Those who are well have no need of a physician, but those who

are sick; I have come not to call the righteous but sinners." (2:17)

In his answer Jesus once again goes to the heart of the matter. Levi was not physically sick. He was a man collaborating with and profiting by the unjust systems of the world of his time. He represented the sickness of the world in which he lived, continued in the sickness of the world in which *we* live.

In choosing to align himself with Jesus, the healer, Levi was stepping from the old into the new. It is a step all followers of Jesus are asked to take. All of us are asked to shake off our paralysis, take up our mat, and walk the new path to our home in God.

When Jesus forgives the paralytic his sins he addresses him with the Greek word *teknon*. The Scripture version used in this book (NRSV) translates that word as "son." But the Greek term does not mean simply "son." It is an affectionate form of address that can also be translated as "my child," "my friend," "my little one," or "my dear."

Thus Jesus speaks to us all: "My little one, your sins are forgiven. You are healed. Go and walk!"

FOR REFLECTION

- What are the habits, attitudes, addictions, or behaviors that paralyze you and keep you from Jesus?

- Reflect on what it means to you that Jesus addresses you as he did the paralytic, calling you *teknon*, my little one, my friend, my dear. Now consider the fact that he relates in the same way to all those with whom you live and work and co-exist.

EVENING PRAYER
Dear Jesus, let the forgiveness you offer
and the newness you bring help me renew my life. Amen.

THIRD DAY

"Is it lawful to do good on the Sabbath?"

Read Mark 2:18—3:19

The conflict around Jesus is beginning to grow. He is being criticized for his outreach to sinners. He has forgiven the sins of the paralytic and cured him of his infirmity. He has wined and dined with a tax collector. When he announces his mission, "The time is fulfilled...repent, and believe in the good news," he is obviously calling for an end to the existing situation and the beginning of a new era. Many of the people, especially the religious leaders, feel threatened by this.

The scribes and Pharisees accused Jesus of socializing with sinners. In their accusations, they tried to curtail God's love. They felt that God would not reach out to sinners. If you did not stick to the rules and regulation, which to a great extent they themselves had drawn up and imposed on others, you were "out."

That is why they begin to challenge Jesus. Why didn't his disciples keep the fast? It was one of the many "why" questions they would ask him throughout his ministry. "Why does this fellow speak in this way?" (2:7); "Why does he eat with tax collectors and sinners?" (2:16).

Jesus' answers were always the same: something new has started; the time has come; the kingdom of God has arrived. The prophets of old had promised that this would happen one day. They had used the metaphor of God coming as a bridegroom, with God's people being the bride (Hosea 2:16; Isaiah 54:5; 62:4-5). Those days had arrived; the bridegroom had come. Why fast while he is here?

Jesus adds images and examples to illustrate the newness of his mission by contrasting it with the old—a new patch on an old garment; new wine in an old wineskin—indicating that he understands the difficulty in accepting what he teaches.

But many do not want to give up the old; they do not want to believe in the new. More accurately, perhaps, they want to believe in the new without giving up the old. No way, says Jesus. God's unconditional love is all there is in the new order.

We should be careful not to be too quick to blame the Pharisees for their faulty thinking. We too may be suffering from the same misunderstanding. Are we not inclined to curtail God's unconditional love as well? An example might illustrate this point.

While planning an eight-day retreat for a large community of religious sisters, the retreat master asked their coordinator whether there was anything in particular that he should be aware of. After some hesitation, she replied: "Yes, tell them that God loves them. Some of them really need to hear that. Too many consider themselves sinners and are afraid of God."

Here is another example. A woman had a friend who became very sick. She visited her friend in the hospital and, noticing her pain, she put her hand on her friend's shoulder. When she withdrew her hand, the friend asked, "Please put your hand back; it takes my pain away." The woman was shaken by this comment and left the room in a hurry, thinking, "This is impossible, I can't have healing power. I am a sinful person. It is impossible."

How often do we hear others say, "I am only a simple human being"? How often do we say this ourselves? Why do we curtail the unconditional love of God, and limit who we are called to be?

Motivated by their fear, the critics of Jesus continue to harass him. They noticed that some of Jesus' disciples had been plucking heads of wheat on the Sabbath and eating the grains. Harvesting was forbidden on that day according to the law of Moses (Exodus 34:21). So, again the Pharisees ask "why"; why did Jesus allow his disciples to do something like that in his presence? Jesus answers them in a kind of teasing way by referring to what David and his soldiers did when they were hungry and broke a law in order to eat. Then he adds what reads like a riddle:

"The Sabbath was made for humankind, and not humankind for the Sabbath; so the Son of Man is lord even of the Sabbath" (2:27–28).

Jesus then solves this riddle when he enters a synagogue and heals a man with a withered hand. His opponents were there as well, and they watched to see whether he would cure on the Sabbath. If he did, they would be able to accuse him once again of disregarding the law.

Down through the centuries, the man with the withered hand has intrigued biblical scholars. Most of them think that the man was a mason who had had an accident on the job. They suggest that a stone had fallen on his hand, crushing it and taking away his livelihood.

Full of compassion for the man, Jesus calls him: "Come forward!" All the eyes in the synagogue must have been fixed on him. Then Jesus looks around and asks, "Is it lawful to do good or to do harm on the Sabbath, to save life or to kill?" When no one answers, he looks around "with anger…grieved at their hardness of heart." Then he asks the man to stretch out his hand, and he is healed.

In the new order, in God's community, each and every human being is more important than a liturgical rule. The final authority is love, not law. But the religious and political defenders of the status quo did not agree. They left the synagogue in protest, and met together to discuss "how to destroy him" (3:6).

FOR REFLECTION

- Have you ever used a regulation or law to avoid helping some-one in need?

- Did you ever apologize to someone by saying "I am only a human being"? Do you feel this statement has validity in view of God's unconditional love? Why or why not?

- When speaking about his relation to the law Jesus calls himself "Son of Man." He does that often in Mark's gospel (2:10, 28; 8:31, 38; 9:9, 12,31; 10:33, 45; 13:26; 14:21, 41:62). Why do you think Jesus calls himself that?

MORNING PRAYER

Almighty God, you brought your son into our world to restore it.
Help us share in his zeal for renewal. Amen.

FAITH RESPONSE FOR TODAY

Break one of your self-imposed rules or customs in order to pay better attention to the needs of someone near to you.

EVENING MEDITATION

"Whoever does the will of God is my brother and sister and mother."

Read Mark 3:20–35

When his family learns about the rumblings being made against him and the crowds whose constant presence does not even give him time to eat, they go to bring Jesus home. Even his mother is there with them. Meanwhile, scribes from Jerusalem arrive and accuse Jesus of being in cahoots with Beelzebub, the name they gave to the ruler of devils and demons.

Jesus defends himself against the accusation of the scribes. First he makes it clear that this would be nonsense: "How can Satan cast out Satan?" (3:23). Mark writes that he speaks to them in parables, explaining that a house divided against itself would fall apart. He then adds a further parable:

"But no one can enter a strong man's house and plunder his property without first tying up the strong man, then indeed the house can be plundered" (3:27).

It is the kind of riddle we have encountered before in Mark's gospel. What does Jesus really mean? Is he suggesting that he himself is the strong man? Does this refer to his own power, that which John the baptizer had stated was stronger than John's? Did this imply that he knew he would be arrested, bound, and crucified?

Or does the strong man in the story represent the devil, who must be overcome before the good news of God's kingdom could prevail in this world? Jesus does not give the name "devil" to the strong man. But in the context of his time many of his listeners might have assumed that this was who he was referring to in this brief parable.

We might also consider the strong man as representative of the dark forces that terrorize our world and all who live on it: materialism, racism, greed, egoism, fascism, exploitation of the poor, disrespect for nature, and unfair trade relations, to name only a few. These dark forces were the "wild beasts" Jesus met in the desert, where he retreated after his baptism (1:13). There, Jesus had proved to be the more powerful.

Mark refers to this throughout his gospel, portraying the demons whom Jesus meets as terrified by him. At their first encounter, in the synagogue of Capernaum, the unclean spirits in the obsessed man shout: "Have you come to destroy us?" Indeed, that is exactly what Jesus had come to do.

Jesus has power over all the forces that threaten and oppress people, and he invites his disciples to join in that struggle. This fight is not directed against human persons as such, but is a struggle against all that is sinful and evil in us and in others.

Having faced the scribes from Jerusalem and having warned them that it would be unforgivable not to recognize the Spirit of God in him, Jesus is confronted by the delegation from his family. Mark does not mention her by name, but he notes that even Jesus' mother was with them. (Had they forced her to come?) They come to bring him home because they had heard all kinds of rumors about Jesus. People were even saying of him: "He has gone out of his mind."

Jesus was in a room with a crowd all around him, as usual. His family remained standing outside but sent in a message for him: "Your mother and your brothers and sisters are outside, asking for you."

It was the same kind of question Jesus had heard before, when Simon and some others had hunted for him in Capernaum while he was at prayer: "Everyone is searching for you." He had refused to come then because he could not allow himself to be circled-in by the people of Capernaum. He had to proclaim the good news to the neighboring villages. The kingdom of God was for all!

Jesus has a similar reaction to his family's request. He makes it clear that there are more important ties than those of one's natural family. And so he does not leave the room to see his family but asks the people around him: "Who are my brothers and sisters?" Answering his own question, he looks at those around him and says:

"Here are my brothers and sisters. Whoever does the will of God is my brother and sister and mother" (3:34–35).

This does not mean that caring for your family is not important. Doing so is obviously God's will, as indicated by the ten commandments. Parents should take care of their children, and children should honor their father and mother. Family bonds should be respected and valued. This is what motivated Jesus' family in coming to rescue him; they came because they were concerned about him.

What they did not understand, like so many others, was the new order Jesus had come to introduce: the kingdom of God. In this place we are all God's family, each of us loved in the same way by the one Jesus calls Father.

FOR REFLECTION

- What would your life be like if the realization of the kingdom of God was its guiding principle?

- Jesus stated that those who do God's will are "my brother, my sister and my mother." Notice that he does not mention "father." Reflect on the significance of this omission, which indicates that for Jesus (and for all of us) there is only one Father, who is in heaven.

- Jesus not only casts out the evil spirits who terrorize this world, he also considered the fight against disease as a critical part of his mission. How can you join him in this struggle, especially within a global context?

EVENING PRAYER

Almighty God, help me to respond wholeheartedly
to the liberating and healing presence of your Son. Amen.

FOURTH DAY

"Other seed fell into good soil and brought forth grain"

Read Mark 4:1–33

Jesus sat down in a boat, with the lake as his backdrop. Thus he began to teach the crowd in front of him on the beach, telling them the parable of the sower and the seed.

When the crowd had dispersed, Jesus sat with his disciples, who asked Jesus why he so often spoke in parables. Why couldn't he be more straightforward? Why didn't he just announce, determine, and define things? Jesus replies by saying "To you has been given the secret of the kingdom of God, but for those outside, everything comes in parables" (4:11). He then proceeded to explain the parable of the sower and the seed to those gathered there.

Time and time again, Jesus uses parables to put across his point. Perhaps he did so because he suspected that if he used a more direct approach to announce the good news he would meet with resistance. But there may have been a different reason he used parables, namely, out of respect for his listeners. The great advantage of telling parables is that their interpretation is left to the listener.

A Kenyan professor at St. Paul University in Nairobi once commented that he liked the way the preachers at the chapel there used stories in their sermons. "Yet," he added, "I have one difficulty. Too often, these preachers explain their stories after they have been told. Our African storytellers would never do that." When asked to explain what he meant, the professor himself told a story .

It seems he had caught his young son telling a lie, and he wanted to warn him not to that again. The professor could have told his son that it is sinful to lie, or that nobody in his family ever lied (which most likely was a lie itself). Instead, he told his son a well-known story about a boy named Johnny, who spent his days shepherding goats for his grandparents. Shepherding can be very lonely, and so on two occasions Johnny had shouted in the direction of the village: "Lion, lion!" But there was no lion at all; Johnny simply wanted some company. Twice the villagers had run out to help him, but when they found out there was no lion they headed back home, saying, "Johnny is a liar." Then one day, there was a *real* lion, and Johnny again shouted, "Lion, lion!" But no one went to help him, because he had lied twice before. And Johnny was never seen again.

After he had finished this story, the professor told his son, "Good night!" He left him to make up his own mind and draw the conclusions by himself.

Jesus only explains his parables when his disciples ask him for that explanation. He would prefer to leave the interpretation up to them. He insists: "Let anyone with ears to hear listen!"

The sower and seed parables offer multiple possibilities for interpretation. Each is full of powerful symbols and imagery: a sower, seed, earth, rocks, thorns, a grandiose yield and no yield at all, germination, growth, the harvest, the small mustard seed, the greatest of shrubs, large branches, the birds of heaven, and the kingdom of God made manifest.

Let us meditate for a moment on the relationship between a seed and the earth. Left alone, out of the ground, a seed can do nothing. It has to be put in earth to grow. Now apply this imagery to yourself. As the earth receives the seed, nurtures it, and eventually gives birth to a plant, we too must accept the good news within ourselves, nurture it, and give birth to the reign of God. Within us lies the capacity and the power to make the seed of the kingdom grow.

The process of conversion and a willingness to listen prepares the soil to receive the word. But we must continue onward to a consequent development, a discovery, a disclosure, an epiphany of the power breathed into us by God from the very beginning of our existence. In hearing Jesus, in listening to him we discover ourselves.

With the parables of the sower and seed, Jesus expresses not only his disappointment that some will not have the ears to hear his words. At the same time, he shares his hope and his firm belief in the final outcome of the good news: the new order, the alternative world, the kingdom of God he had come to introduce. Indeed, as often as the seed would fall on dead, dried-up, and unwilling soil it would also fall on good soil and grow.

This hopeful confidence, a dimension of the Spirit within him, was the tonic and the fuel that kept Jesus going. To the twelve he had chosen Jesus explained that you do not bring in a lamp to hide it under a basket or a bed to show that there is to be nothing kept secret. He repeated what he had said before: "Let anyone with ears to hear listen."

A willingness to listen to someone is always an expression of love, a hope that our relationship with him or her will become deeper and better. We must be like the good earth. If we lose contact with Jesus and do not listen to his word, his message will wither and dry up for lack of the good soil only we can provide.

FOR REFLECTION

- Reflect on the parable of the sower and the seed (4:3–8), as well as on Jesus' interpretation of this parable (4:14–20). What type of soil do you see yourself as?

- How well is the word of God growing within you? How do you nurture the soil and the seed so that the kingdom can be born through you?

MORNING PRAYER

Dear Jesus, may your words take flesh in my life
and shine forth in my actions. Amen.

FAITH RESPONSE FOR TODAY

Take some time today to listen to someone close to you whom you may not have had time for recently.

EVENING MEDITATION

"Let us go across to the other side."

Read Mark 4:35—5:20

The twelve did not like to go to the other side of the lake. They wanted to remain on their own side, where they were comfortable. They considered the people on the other side as aliens, pagans.

In Mark's gospel, there are six occasions when Jesus asks his disciples to go with him to the "other side." On one occasion, he "made his disciples get into the boat and go on ahead to the other side (6:45), which sounds as if he was practically forcing them to do so. In truth, we can't blame the disciples for being hesitant: every time they go with Jesus to the other side, something happens along the way.

The worst case was when Jesus asked the disciples to go to Gerasa, home to the Gerasenes. They left in the evening, after Jesus had told them, "Let us go to the other side." Those disciples who were fishermen might have known that a storm was brewing as they set out. Did they mention this to Jesus? If they did, he did not show any concern. That may be the reason that the text adds rather tellingly, "they took him with them in the boat, just as he was" (4:36).

Jesus lay down on a cushion in the stern of the boat, the place where the navigator stood. He slept as the storm gained force and began to swamp the boat. He slept until the disciples woke him up, shouting, "Teacher, do you not care that we are perishing?" (4:38).

Have you ever said something similar when you were in physical, psychological, or some other sort of danger? Have you ever seen people in distress or in trouble cry out, "Where is God? Has God forgotten us?"

Jesus woke up, and the first thing he did was calm the storm, rebuking the wind and ordering the water of the lake: "Peace! Be still!" He then turned to his disciples in the boat, who were filled with awe at what they had seen him do, and said: "Why are you afraid? Have you still no faith?" In a way they answered his question in the negative, for they asked each other, "Who then is this, that even the wind and the sea obey him?" The disciples did not yet know who Jesus really was.

After these many years—more than two thousand, in fact—do *we* really know who Jesus is and what role he wishes to play in our lives? Don't we too often doubt and have reservations about our commitment to follow Jesus?

Once they are safely at the other side, the twelve encounter a new crisis. They had been afraid to go to the other side; they were reluctant to meet the people who lived there. But they could not have imagined what they saw as soon as they stepped out of their boat: a man emerging out of a tomb. The man, possessed by a legion of evil spirits, "immediately" confronts them. They could not have met a person more frightening and alien to them than this one. He was a pagan (an encounter with whom was forbidden for any upright Jew of those days); he lived in a pagan cemetery (another taboo); and he was situated next to a herd of pigs, which were considered unclean by Jews. The man had been exiled by his compatriots, chained and shackled; but he had broken loose, and no one had been able to restrain him. Day and night he howled like a wild animal, bruising himself with stones. In the minds of the disciples, this man was evil personified.

The demon recognized Jesus and remembered how Jesus had overcome it in the desert. It shouted, "Do not torment me!" When Jesus ordered it to come out, it did not do so. Jesus then asked its name, just as exorcists would do nowadays. The demon replied, "My name is Legion; for we are many." The demons ask to be sent into the nearby herd of pigs, and Jesus "gave them permission" to do so. And as the demons entered them, the pigs rushed down into the lake and drowned.

Those in charge of the pigs ran off to tell their story to the villagers, who hurried to find Jesus. They were alarmed to see him sitting with the man recently released from the demon's grip, properly dressed and in his right mind. Upset and not understanding what had happened, the villagers asked Jesus to leave.

This strange story well illustrates what Jesus came to do for the world, that is, to help us overcome the evil that terrorizes it. The story is full of hints and symbols that were better understood by those who first heard it. Take, for example, the name the evil in the possessed man gives itself. It is Legion, the Roman name for a battalion of about 2,000 soldiers. Was this name meant to refer to the violent occupation of the region at the time, judged by the Jews as evil? Did it remind the Roman Christians to whom the story was told of the Roman authority that persecuted them as well? These are intriguing questions, ones that scholars have been mulling over since the gospel was first told.

The kingdom Jesus came to introduce in this world is open to all. It is not restricted to a small circle of "saved ones," either then or now. The kingdom is on this side of the lake, but it is also on the other side; it is destined to be here, there, and everywhere.

What happened to the man dispossessed of the demon? He asked to be allowed to "be with Jesus." But Jesus refuses, saying, "Go home to your friends and tell them how much the Lord has done for you, and what mercy he has shown you." This man, who had been practically the embodiment of evil, became the first one to proclaim Jesus in the non-Hebrew world: "And he went away and began to proclaim in the Decapolis how much Jesus had done for him, and everyone was amazed" (5:19–20).

The disciples returned home as well. Jesus had opened up a whole new world to them.

FOR REFLECTION

- Have you ever prayed, "God, why have you forgotten me?" What answer did you receive?

- Reflect on the fact that Jesus does not fight the people who are obsessed by evil, but fights the evil in them.

- What is your response to those who are terrorized by evil? Do you reject them, or do you show mercy to them?

EVENING PRAYER

Dear Jesus, you are gentle, humble, and merciful of heart.
Help me to follow your example in my relationships with others. Amen.

FIFTH DAY

MORNING MEDITATION

"Give them something to eat."

Read Mark 6:6—8:10

Chasing demons and curing the sick does not help the world very much if the health is not sustained and nourished.

In any discussion about raising the standard of living for the entire world, the provision of food for all is a fundamental issue. As long as there are people starving in our world, something is wrong; restoration and healing are needed.Eating is necessary to maintain life, and it is also a condition for ensuring peace. Eating together is a sign and symbol of belonging.

In recent years Asian bishops and theologians have insisted on the need for interreligious dialogue between the rich Christian West and the poor Hindu/Muslim East. They add that such dialogue would not need to take place if the poverty and subsequent hunger so present in their part of the world was realistically addressed and attended to.

It is no wonder that food plays such an important role in Jesus' outreach to others. Bread itself is often mentioned in Mark's gospel. In the section you read at the beginning of this meditation, bread in one or another form is mentioned eighteen times! The first time is when the disciples are sent out. Jesus tells them "to take nothing for their journey except a staff; no bread, no bag, no money in their belts" (6:8). This meant that the disciples would have to depend totally on the ones to whom they were sent for sustenance. They were going to be guests. It was definitely a good way to keep them focused on the significance of their message.

After the death of John the Baptist, the disciples return from their mission, full of enthusiasm. Jesus tells them, "Come away to a deserted place all by yourselves and rest a while" (6:31). Though they leave by boat, the crowd finds out. In no time they are surrounded by thousands of people, whom Jesus begins to teach. As the day moves toward evening, the disciples tell Jesus to send the crowds away so that they may find something to eat. But Jesus tells them, "You give them something to eat."

Though protesting, the disciples find two fish and five loaves of bread. Jesus, "looking up to heaven"—words that are preserved in the consecration during Eucharist—blesses the food, asks the people to sit down, and gives the bread and fish to his disciples, who begin to distribute them to the crowd. There is more than enough for everyone; in the end, the leftovers fill twelve baskets. (Perhaps the twelve baskets of leftovers indicate Jesus' intention to feed the twelve tribes of Israel.)

Later that night, the disciples are "on the sea," going to Bethsaida. Jesus has stayed behind to pray. But when Jesus looks out on the lake, and sees that there is a strong wind working against the boat, he begins to walk toward the disciples—right over the water! They see him, and cry out in terror; none of the miracles they have seen to this time has prepared them for this. "Immediately" Jesus says to them, "Take heart, it is I, do not be afraid." But their hearts were hardened, for "they did not understand about the loaves" (6:50–52).

As the gospel continues, we see the scribes and Pharisees challenging Jesus on the way his disciples and followers eat—without washing their hands or their food. Jesus responds that foods cannot be unclean in a religious sense; only persons can. Then he in turn challenges the pharisaic custom that allows them to refuse to care for their aged parents. Again we see what is the bottom line for Jesus: human needs come before rules.

At home again, his disciples ask Jesus for a further explanation of the question of unclean food. He criticizes them for not understanding him, and declares all foods clean, for "it is what comes out of a person that defiles" (7:20). This is one of Jesus' clearest statements declaring the old is over and the new begun.

Jesus then proceeds to cite a series of attitudes that make people unclean from within: "fornication, theft, murder, adultery, avarice, wickedness, deceit, licentiousness, envy, slander, pride, folly."

Food remains an issue in the next event reported by Mark. A stranger, a Syro-Phoenician woman, meets Jesus on the other side of the lake, in the pagan region of Tyre. She asks Jesus to heal her daughter, but he tells her: "Let the children be fed first, for it is not fair to take the children's food and throw it to the dogs" (7:27). The woman does not seem to be offended by the distinction Jesus makes between his people and hers. Instead, she picks up his metaphor by saying that the dogs *do* join the meal by eating the crumbs under the table. Jesus is amazed, and he heals her daughter.

The final story in this morning's gospel passage is a repeat of what had happened earlier. This time the disciples found seven loaves and a few fish. Jesus gave thanks, broke the bread and divided the fish, and gave them to his disciples to distribute. All ate "and were filled." The leftovers were collected, filling seven baskets. First twelve, now seven.

And is not seven the number symbolizing and indicating completeness, the whole of humanity, the feeding and restoring of all?

FOR REFLECTION

- What does it mean for you to sit at table with Jesus?

- Jesus responds to the Syro-Phoenician woman and heals her daughter. How do you respond when others come to you in need?

MORNING PRAYER
Almighty God, give us this day our daily bread!

FAITH RESPONSE FOR TODAY
In one way or another, do something to offer help to the starving in our world. One way to do so is to visit www.thehungersite.com on the Internet. Every time you log on to this site a bowl of rice is donated to an agency that helps the hungry.

EVENING MEDITATION

"The Son of Man came...
to give his life as a ransom for many."

Read Mark 8:11—10:45

In the beginning all seemed to go well. There was every reason to think that Jesus would succeed in his mission to bring about the reign of God. Consider how simple it was for him to engage the twelve disciples in ministry. Look at his miracles, the exorcised demons, the enthusiasm of the crowds who surrounded him, and the enormous provision of food for the hungry.

Yet resistance to Jesus was increasing. He was not understood, and he suffered for this. The Pharisees came to ask him for a sign from heaven, and he "sighed deeply in his spirit and said, 'Why does this generation ask for a sign?'" Wasn't his very presence enough of a sign?

On one of their boat trips, Jesus warned his disciples to be aware of malicious "yeast" of the Pharisees and of Herod, who killed John the Baptist. But the disciples, too, did not understand him. They thought he was cautioning them because they did not have bread for the journey. No, Jesus replies. This was not about a lack of bread; had they forgotten how he had fed the crowds twice before?

Landing near Bethsaida, a blind man is brought to Jesus. He heals him in two stages as if to show the disciples what should happen to their own blindness. When Jesus first touches him, the man sees vaguely. It is only after lays hands on his eyes a second time that he sees everything clearly.

Jesus then tests the twelve, asking, "Who do you say that I am?" Peter answers for them all: "You are the Messiah." Peter saw, but only vaguely; the first stage. He was not mistaken in believing that Jesus was the Messiah; but he was mistaken in his expectations of the role the

Messiah would play in the world. For too many Jews that role meant the restoration of their nation, the undoing of Roman occupation, and the assurance of economic prosperity. Peter did not yet understand that Jesus had come to restore the world by introducing the reign of God. He did not as yet see clearly; he needed further healing.

When Jesus begins to explain that he, as the Son of Man, would undergo great suffering and die—though he would rise again after three days—Peter vehemently objects. He had not joined with Jesus for suffering, pain, and death! Jesus sharply reproaches Peter:

Get behind me, Satan! For you are setting your mind not on divine things but on human things (8:33).

Turning to his disciples and the others who were following him, he adds that those who try to save their own lives will lose them; God's kingdom will prevail.

Many biblical commentators call these events a turning point in Mark's gospel, the moment of truth. The disciples who had followed Jesus guided by their own hopes and dreams were here confronted by the reality of his life and mission. It signaled the process of conversion that each of his disciples down through the ages must face. The price for sharing in the kingdom of God would have to be paid, but the outcome was guaranteed.

Six days later, Jesus takes Peter, James, and John with him up the mountain to pray. There the disciples see him in his transfigured glory, in the company of Elijah and Moses. Once again, Peter misunderstands what has happened. He indicates that he wants to stay there, and says, "Rabbi, it is good for us to be here; let us make three dwellings, one for you, one for Moses, and one for Elijah."Then a voice from heaven answers him, "This is my Son, the Beloved; listen to him" (9:5-7).

This misunderstanding of Jesus' intention is still seen today. Television preachers often play on people's false hopes, that faithfulness to Jesus and God will bring about human desires, such as wealth and prosperity.

Some years ago a book was published called *The Prayer of Jabez*. It is based on a short incident in the first book of Chronicles:

Jabez called on the God of Israel, saying, "Oh that you would bless me and enlarge my border, and that your hand might be with me, and that you would keep me from hurt and harm!" And God granted what he asked (1 Chr 4:10).

By stressing the first part of the prayer, the impression was given that one could find a way to wealth through faith in God. The book became a phenomenal bestseller; more than nine million copies have been sold since its publication. We might wonder if the eager readers of that text have made the same mistake that Peter and the other eleven did when they assumed that following Jesus would bring about only good, ignoring the suffering and pain that would come with discipleship.

Mark notes one misunderstanding about Jesus after the other. Jesus blames the disciples for their lack of faith and prayer when they tried in vain to heal a sick boy; for quarreling among themselves about who would be the greatest; for their envy when they hear about someone else who healed in Jesus' name; and for not understanding what he told them about marital fidelity and about the difficulty rich people would have in entering the kingdom of God.

Jesus then takes a little child into his arms and tells the disciples: "Whoever welcomes one such child in my name welcomes me, and whoever welcomes me welcomes not me but the one who sent me" (9:37). We must embrace God's rule as Jesus embraced the child he took up in his arms that day.

Later in this passage, the children are brought before Jesus again—though the disciples try to prevent this from happening. He tells them in no uncertain terms:

Let the little children come to me; do not stop them; for it is to such as these that the kingdom of God belongs (10:14).

Truly, if we cannot be like children, trusting and innocent in our acceptance of the Father, we cannot hope to gain the kingdom.

As this passage closes, Jesus encounters a rich man who asks what he must do to enter the kingdom. Jesus' response to the man could have been no more shocking that it would be to us today, sated as we are with materialism:

Go, sell what you own, and give the money to the poor, and you will have treasure in heaven; then come, follow me (10:21).

Our passage this morning offers two difficult challenges that each of us must face if we are to inherit the kingdom and share in the eternal life of Christ: to put our very lives on the line in order to gain eternal life, and to reconsider our relationship to whatever we own.

Are you ready to consider these changes in your life? Can you truly afford to say "no" to what Jesus asks?

FOR REFLECTION

- Have you ever made a sacrifice with an eye toward God's kingdom? What is your experience of Jesus' command to deny yourself, take up your cross, and follow him?

- Are you willing to ask, "Good Teacher, what must I do to inherit eternal life?" and live by the answer you receive in your heart?

EVENING PRAYER

Dear Jesus, help me to understand my place and my role in establishing your Father's kingdom here on earth. Amen.

SIXTH DAY

M O R N I N G   M E D I T A T I O N

"My house shall be called a house of prayer for all the nations"

Read Mark 10:46—11:25

In the midst of all the misunderstandings noted in Mark's gospel, the story of Bartimaeus is like a breath of fresh air. For once all goes well, and Mark wants to stress that point.

Mark calls the blind man Bartimaeus, son of Timaeus. He is dressed in rags, sitting in the gutter, a non-participant in his society, a bystander. Bartimaeus hears the crowd and is told that Jesus is coming through the streets. He begins to shout: "Jesus, son of David, have mercy on me!"

The people surrounding Jesus tell him to be quiet, but this only makes him shout louder. Jesus stops and says, "Call him here." The others call him and say, "Take heart; get up, he is calling you!" Throwing off his cloak, Bartimaeus jumps up and goes right up to Jesus, who asks him, "What do you want me to do for you?" He answers: "My teacher, let me see again!" Jesus says to him, "Go, your faith has made you well." He is healed immediately, regaining his sight, and he follows Jesus to Jerusalem. No longer sitting by the side of the road, Bartimaeus now travels on it.

All of us can identify with Bartimaeus, who represents our blindness, our need, and the only answer to it.

To follow Jesus at this point in the story means to be on the way to Jerusalem. This is where he himself foretold that he would be betrayed, handed over to the authorities, put to death by the Romans, and rise again after three days (10:34).

When Jesus reaches Jerusalem riding on a borrowed colt, the people enthusiastically welcome him. He first goes to the temple, then heads to Bethany to spend the night there. The next morning, on his way back to the temple, Jesus sees a fig tree without any fruit, and he curses it: "May no one ever eat fruit from you again" (11:14). This symbolic gesture foretells what will happen in the temple.

Upon arriving at the temple, Jesus becomes angry with the commerce taking place within its walls. He overturns the bankers' stalls, and the stands where the doves are being sold. Further, "He would not allow anyone to carry anything through the temple." This meant that the continuous procession of people who walked through the temple on their way to present their offerings to the priests came to a standstill. They must have heard what Jesus said: "My house shall be called a house of prayer for all the nations, but you have made it a den of robbers" (11:15–16).

Jesus' words were a rallying cry to rid the temple of all those who had co-opted it for their own interests. The heart of his fervor for the temple to remain a sacred place lies in the words that Jesus quotes from the prophet Isaiah: "My house shall be called a house of prayer for all nations"(56:7). It was a challenge to open their circle to the whole of humanity, God's family. He called the people to be a light to the nations, but too many were mired in triumphalism and exclusivity.

But Jesus' reminder threatened the temple leadership. Once the temple service had restarted, they came together and "kept looking for a way to kill him; for they were afraid of him, because the whole crowd was spellbound by his teaching" (11:18).

This same call to openness and solidarity might threaten and overwhelm us as well when we realize its religious, social, economic, and even political consequences. Yet the inclusivity asked for by Jesus is of great importance in our day, confronted as we are by interreligious differences. Pope John Paul II stressed this a letter written in 2001, "At the Beginning of a New Millennium." In it he asks us all to accept the challenge of interreligious dialogue, a dialogue, that must continue in our increasingly pluralistic society. He stressed that this is the only sure basis for peace in the wars caused by religious differences (#55).

Several other Church documents not only emphasize this same need for openness, but offer ways on how to realize this. One of the first steps to take is to be good neighbors in our own communities, welcoming each other, organizing simple social gatherings, and helping each other whenever that help might be needed. We might then tackle together common problems we face, from how to clean up our neighborhoods to insuring the safety of our children in the street.

As we do this, we can speak with one another about our inspiration and the reasons for our ministry. In other words, we can share our faith experiences. This would truly plant the seeds of evangelization within our communities, and further the cause of understanding both our religious similarities and our differences.

Jesus tells us in 11:23, "Truly I tell you, if you say to this mountain, 'Be taken up and thrown into the sea,' and if you do not doubt in your heart, but believe that what you say will come to pass, it will be done for you."

FOR REFLECTION

- How do you welcome newcomers to your neighborhood or parish community?

- How effective is the outreach in your faith community? If there is room for improvement, what can you do to promote change?

- What is your response to someone who has given up on the church?

PRAYER SUGGESTION

Lord, bless all those who walk the road that leads
to the heavenly Jerusalem, the city of peace.
Teach us the ways to gather together in your name. Amen.

FAITH RESPONSE FOR TODAY

Actively seek God's presence in those whom you meet today. Try to identify God's goodness in them. Enjoy the unexpected gifts they may offer you.

EVENING MEDITATION

"This is but the beginning of the birth pangs."
Read Mark 11:26—14:9

Mark reports on how the opponents of Jesus have kept to their decision. Slowly they close in on him. The chief priests, scribes, and elders come to challenge him. Who authorized him to do what he did and to teach what he taught? Jesus does not answer them because they do not answer his question: "Did the baptism of John come from heaven, or was it of human origin? Answer me" (11:30).

During those last days in Jerusalem, Jesus told the chief priests, scribes, and elders one of the key parables in Mark's gospel, the parable of the wicked tenants. The story concerns a man who planted a vineyard, leased it to tenants, and went abroad. At harvest time he sent a servant to collect the share of the harvest due to him. But the tenants beat the servant and sent him back emptyhanded. The owner then sent a second servant, whom they beat over his head and insulted. The third servant whom he sent was killed. Many other servants were sent, all of whom were beaten, insulted, or killed. Finally, the landowner sent his beloved son. He said to himself, they will respect him, he is my son. But the wicked tenants said: "'This is the heir; come, let us kill him, and the inheritance will be ours" (12:7).

By then those who were listening knew that this parable was directed toward them, and that Jesus was the beloved son. When Jesus asked them, "What then will the owner of the vineyard do?" the answer was obvious. But he added that the one rejected would become the cornerstone of what was to come. He, the beloved Son, was going to the cornerstone of the kingdom of God.

Next, the Pharisees and Herodians asked Jesus whether it is lawful to pay taxes to the Roman emperor. They were hoping to trick him with this question. When they showed him the Roman coin they used to pay their tax with the head of the emperor stamped on it, he answered them: "Give to the emperor the things that are the emperor's, and to God the things that are God's" (12:17).

A scribe then asked about the most important commandment. In the end, Jesus and the scribe agree:

> The first is… "you shall love the Lord your God with all your heart, and with all your soul, and with all your mind, and with all your strength." The second is this, "You shall love your neighbor as yourself." There is no other commandment greater than these (12:39–41).

Then Jesus said to the scribe, "You are not far from the kingdom of God." But then Jesus goes on to caution the crowd about the scribes:

> Beware of the scribes, who like to walk around in long robes, and to be greeted with respect in the marketplaces, and to have the best seats in the synagogues and places of honor at banquets! They devour widows' houses and for the sake of appearance say long prayers. They will receive the greater condemnation (12:38–40).

As Jesus sat in the temple watching people contribute to the treasury, he noticed a poor widow put two coins in the box. He drew the attention of his disciples to her, admiring and praising her:

> Truly I tell you, this poor widow has put in more than all those who are contributing to the treasury. For all of them have contributed out of their abundance; but she out of her poverty has put in everything she had, all she had to live on (12:43–44).

As they left the temple, one of the disciples comments on the building itself: "Look, Teacher, what large stones and what large buildings!" But Jesus was not impressed, and in fact foretold that one day the temple would be destroyed. Indeed, at the time of his death on the cross the curtain of the temple was torn in two from top to bottom.

Jesus and the disciples go up to the Mount of Olives. Peter, James, John, and Andrew ask him about the destruction of the temple, saying "Tell us, when will this be?" Jesus does not give them a date, but tells them how the temple will be desecrated and destroyed, and how people should try to escape in time from the terrible disaster that would hit Jerusalem.

Jesus then puts the destruction of the temple—which actually took place around the year 70 CE—into a larger context, foreseeing earthquakes, famines, wars, persecutions, betrayals, and false prophets, but also the proclamation of the good news of the kingdom of God to all the nations on earth. To explain all this Jesus used a metaphor best understood by a woman who had given birth. He told the disciples: "This is but the beginning of the birth pangs" (13:8).

This is a very revealing remark, a key statement indicating our situation and position in what is to come. Something is happening. We will be taken up in a process. Even if the situation becomes worse than it is and the sky grows darker, we should not be paralyzed by our fears. These events should foster our hope and endurance.

Jesus assured the disciples and us that after the suffering is over the new will be born in our midst. The pain that comes with shedding the old is an unavoidable condition in giving birth to the new. The Son of Man will appear so that, as Paul would describe the final outcome, "God may be all in all" (1 Cor 15:28). Jesus illustrates this by pointing to a fig tree: "As soon as its branch becomes tender and puts forth its leaves, you know that summer is near." So, he added, "Beware, keep alert" (13:28–33).

In the final section of our gospel reading for this evening, an unnamed woman intuits what is going to happen to Jesus in the next few days. (In John's gospel, the woman is called "Mary," which has led to much speculation over the years about who this "Mary" might be.) Jesus goes to dinner at the house of Simon the leper. While they are eating, the woman comes into the room, bringing with her an alabaster jar filled with nard, an expensive ointment. She breaks the jar and pours the nard over the head of Jesus.

Some who were there became angry that so much money was spent on ointment, money that could have been given to the poor. But Jesus is touched by the woman's gesture. He tells those gathered at table that the poor will always be with them, but he would not. Appreciating the woman's foresight, Jesus defends her:

She has done what she could; she has anointed my body before-

hand for its burial. Truly I tell you, wherever the good news is pro-
claimed in the whole world, what she has done will be told in
remembrance of her (14:8).

FOR REFLECTION

- Does your life and the work you do contribute to the coming of
  God's kingdom here on earth? How and why?

- Jesus reminds us to be aware of the end of our life here on earth.
  Do you make important decisions with this in mind?

- How do you judge the gesture of the woman who spent so much
  money on perfumed oil with which to anoint Jesus?

EVENING PRAYER

Dear Jesus, enlighten me with the grace of the Holy Spirit
so that my life may be filled with justice and peace.
In this way, I will proclaim your mercy to all. Amen.

SEVENTH DAY

MORNING MEDITATION

"Truly this man was God's Son!"

Read Mark 14:10—15:45

Mark's account of Jesus' arrest is as stark as the rest of his gospel. He describes the events as they occur without any avoidance of the betrayal and suffering of the situation. He is mercilessly realistic. Because of this candor his testimony gives us hope. It depicts the human condition and the way that Jesus handled it.

Jesus is aware of what is to come. He tells the disciples: "You will all become deserters" (14:27). Knowing perfectly well that Judas will betray him, Jesus nonetheless invites him, too, to sit at table with the others, and dip his bread into the same bowl. It is indeed a strange and paradoxical situation.

> While they were eating, he took a loaf of bread, and after blessing it he broke it, gave it to them, and said, "Take; this is my body." Then he took a cup, and after giving thanks he gave it to them, and all of them drank from it. He said to them, "This is my blood of the covenant, which is poured out for many. Truly I tell you, I will never again drink of the fruit of the vine until that day when I drink it new in the kingdom of God" (14:22–25).

All who were present ate the bread, his body; they all drank from the wine, his blood. Although they would all desert Jesus in the coming hours, at this moment they were united with him. This ambiguous situation expressed Jesus' willingness to give up his life for them; at the same time, it showed his faith in the work of the Spirit in them.

Jesus even makes an appointment with his disciples: "But after I am raised up, I will go before you to Galilee" (14:28). It would be the moment they would see the kingdom of God come with power, as he had promised them before (Mk 9:1).

After the meal, Jesus and the disciples go to Gethsemane where he asks Peter, James, and John—the disciples who had witnessed his transfiguration—to stay with him. He does nor want to be alone, as he is deeply grieved. Speaking about his death, he asks God, "Abba, Father, for you all things are possible; remove this cup from me; yet, not what I want, but what you want" (14:36).

Praying like this put Jesus in a vulnerable position. He could have escaped his arrest and death. Even once arrested, he would have been able to escape. But to do so would have meant using force, most likely, and Jesus never used violence against other human beings. (When he threw over the bankers' booths and the stands of the dove merchants in the temple, he did so against the object of their evil—profiting by religion—not against the people themselves.)

If Jesus had escaped his fate at that moment, he would have left us no hope. By delivering himself to evil, and letting it do what only it can do, namely kill, he overcame evil while being raised up. Evil and death lost their sting!

When we think about Jesus' sacrifice on the cross, we often forget that his whole life was a sacrifice. Jesus was God; yet he entered into the human condition, taking on all that entailed, in order to redeem humankind from sin and death.

And so Jesus was arrested. Judas kissed him, saying, "Rabbi." One of his disciples (was it Peter?) waved his sword and hit the ear of one of the rabble who had come to arrest him. But then they all fled. One of his disciples even left behind the cloak in which he was dressed, and ran off with the others, naked. Now Jesus was alone.

Brought before the high priests and their entourage, Jesus answered only one question. When he was asked whether he was the Messiah, the Son of God, the blessed one, he answered in the positive: "I am," adding that they would see him returning in power. At this they condemned to death for blasphemy.

Peter, who gone to the courtyard outside the chambers of the high priest, there denied Jesus three times. When he understood what he had done, fulfilling Jesus' prophecy that all would desert him—Peter had asserted, "Even though all become deserters, I will not" (14:29)— he broke down and wept.

Beaten up and ridiculed, Jesus was brought to Pilate the morning after his arrest. He hardly spoke, again answering only one question: was he the King of the Jews? He replied, "You say so."

Pilate understood the local jealousies, and realized the motives of the Jews in trying to put Jesus to death. He tried to save Jesus by giving the Jews a choice between freedom for Jesus, and freedom for Barabbas, a known murderer and insurrectionist. But the crowd chose Barabbas.

Now Pilate had no choice but to place Jesus in the hands of executioners. They mocked him, beat him up, and made him carry his own cross to the place of crucifixion. They forced a passerby, Simon from Cyrene, to help Jesus carry his cross, and then they crucified him.

Jesus refused the palliative they wanted to give him. As he hung on the cross, he was mocked by priests and passersby: "Aha! You who would destroy the temple and build it in three days, save yourself, and come down from the cross!" (15:29–30). Jesus began to pray the words from Psalm 22: "My God, my God, why have your forsaken me?" His prayer expressed the hopeful expectation that God would come to his aid and vindicate his oppressors.

His prayer was heard. A man carrying a sponge drenched in wine ran up to Jesus as he breathed his last breath. At that, the temple curtain split in two from top to bottom. A centurion watching over the crucifixion was heard to say: "Truly this man was God's Son."

Where are the eleven disciples as Jesus dies? Are they hiding in fear? They have done what Jesus predicted would happen, that all who were present at the last supper together would desert him.

The only ones who remain at the crucifixion are some women disciples: "Mary Magdalene, and Mary the mother of James the younger and of Joses, and Salome," along with "many other women who had come up with him to Jerusalem" (15:40–41). They stay and watch as Joseph of Arimathea, a man who was " waiting expectantly for the kingdom of God," takes the body of Jesus down from the cross and buries him.

Could this be all that remains of Jesus' life here on earth?

FOR REFLECTION

- What does it mean to you to receive the body and blood of Christ? How does Eucharist affect your life?

- Jesus promises his disciples that he will see them again even though he knows that they will abandon him in his hour of need. What does this mean to you?

MORNING PRAYER

Dear Jesus, you lived, suffered, died, and rose from the dead
so that we might have eternal life with you.
Have mercy on me, and teach me to follow your ways. Amen.

FAITH RESPONSE FOR TODAY

Take time to meditate on Jesus' betrayal, death, and burial. This would be a good time to receive the sacrament of reconciliation, followed, if possible, by celebrating the Eucharist.

EVENING MEDITATION

"He has been raised!"

Read Mark 16:1–8

We have come to the end of a book that calls itself a beginning. In the final scene of this book, it is early in the morning. As soon as the sun rises and the Sabbath is over, some of the women who had witnessed Jesus' death are going to his tomb. They had brought with them the necessary spices and oils to clean and anoint him properly, according to their customs.

No disciples have come along as the women prepare to pay their last respects. Perhaps the disciples felt that everything had ended in tragedy; perhaps they stayed away for fear that what had happened to Jesus might happen to them. The three women who came to the tomb—Mary Magdalene, Mary, the mother of James, and Salome—may have felt the same way. But they ignored their feelings and came for a proper closure to their relationship with Jesus.

On their way, their overriding worry was, who will role away the stone from the entrance of the tomb for us? But upon arriving there, they discovered that the stone was already rolled back.

At the entrance to the tomb there was a young man dressed in a white robe and sitting on the right, who told them:

Do not be alarmed; you are looking for Jesus of Nazareth, who was crucified. He has been raised; he is not here. Look, there is the place where they laid him. But go, tell his disciples and Peter that he is going ahead of you to Galilee; there you will see him, just as he told you (16:6–7).

And then follows the final line in Mark's book, entitled "The Beginning of the Good News of Jesus the Christ, the Son of God":

So they went out and fled from the tomb, for terror and amazement had seized them; and they said nothing to anyone, for they were afraid.

This ending is so strange and puzzling that it is followed by another "canonical" ending, less abrupt but added on later by someone else.

At first reading Mark seems to leave us with one of his riddles, with a final challenge to the reader. There are in fact a whole set of explanations that might help us to understand Mark's intention.

The young man dressed in white, described as an angel would be visualized in those days, summarizes in a few words what the good news had been about up to that moment. He tells the women that he knows they are looking for Jesus of Nazareth, who was crucified and who has been raised. He also points to the empty place where Jesus had been buried. This emptiness frightens them. All kinds of things might have happened to Jesus' body since his burial.

The angel tells the women that they must tell the disciples and Peter that Jesus is going to keep the appointment he had made with them earlier: "But after I am raised up, I will go before you to Galilee" (14:28).

The women had seen an empty tomb; they had not seen the risen Lord. And so they reacted with fear because they did not understand.

This leads us to a second explanation of Mark's ending. His book, a collection of stories about what Jesus had done and taught, and about how the people around him had reacted, was written to be read to the first Christian communities At that time, this community was persecuted throughout most of the Roman empire. Now just imagine that this book would end with the story of the panicky exit made by the first visitors to Jesus' tomb. Wouldn't those hearing this ending jump up, protest, and say, "That is not the end: the disciples *did* meet Jesus in Galilee! They saw him, and Peter was there!"

The early Christians had all been witnesses to the power of the Risen Lord and of his Spirit in their own lives and in the lives of fellow believers. Their experiences, described in books such as the Acts of the Apostles, made that very clear.

But on that first morning after Jesus' death, the women had not yet encountered the Risen Lord. And so they went to the tomb simply out of the goodness of their hearts. No wonder they were so distressed to see that Jesus' body was not where they thought it would be. It is only natural that the empty tomb was bad news for them at that moment.

We can surmise that Mark intended to end his work as a challenge to his readers to uncover the experience of the Risen Lord in their own lives. Mark had called his gospel "The Beginning of the Good News," the beginning of God's kingdom, of God's rule, of the civilization of love, of a world steeped in justice and peace. This was the world people came to find when John the Baptizer began to announce its coming.

Everyone of us is called to that appointment in Galilee, to meet the risen Lord, and to hear from his own mouth the words: "Repent and believe in the good news."

FOR REFLECTION

- One way to look at the abrupt ending of Mark's gospel is to see it as an invitation to react in a way different from the women at the tomb. As this retreat comes to a close, how do you react to the ending of Mark's gospel?

- It is within the community of faithful disciples that we find the Risen Lord. What does this mean to you? How do you experience this reality in your everyday life?

- Mark's gospel not only tells a story, but also offers a challenge. It asks us to set our minds on what is divine rather than on what is human. Are you willing to begin living your life this way?

EVENING PRAYER

Risen Lord, raise me to life.
Set me on fire with your Spirit.
Fill all of us with your glory,
and bring us to life everlasting, Amen.

CONCLUSION

There remains one intriguing question to be answered. If Jesus overcame evil by his life, death and resurrection, why is there still so much left for us to do? It is a difficult and serious issue.

Mark's gospel implies an answer to this issue. He tells us that Jesus overcame evil in the desert. The battle was won. The evil spirits Jesus encounters later are afraid of him; they ask him again and again to leave them alone. Though the final victory has been won, there is still work to be done. Jesus does this starting with his first exorcism in Capernaum. Sending his disciples out in the world, he engages them—and subsequently, us—in the task.

Jesus could have eliminated evil in one fell swoop, but in that case we would not have been involved in the process. We would have been treated like small children for whom everything is done. Now we are engaged. At the end, when we "see 'the Son of Man coming in clouds' with great power and glory," and we will be gathered "from the four winds and the ends of the earth to the ends of heaven" (13:26–27), we will be able to say together with Jesus, the Christ, "We did it!"

We have read that Jesus speaks about "the beginning of the birth pangs" (13:8). The "old" at this moment is giving birth to the new. The situation in our world might even become worse than it is at the moment. But even that, Jesus tells us, is a sign that we are nearer to the promised glory.

The opposition and plotting around Jesus culminated in his death on the cross, and it was immediately followed by the manifestation of his glory! This is the hope inherent in Mark's gospel. His message will help us to endure whatever is to come, together with Christ.

MY JOURNAL

MY JOURNAL

_____
_____
_____
_____
_____
_____
_____
_____
_____
_____
_____
_____
_____
_____
_____
_____
_____
_____
_____
_____
_____
_____
_____
_____
_____
_____
_____
_____
_____

MY JOURNAL

_____
_____
_____
_____
_____
_____
_____
_____
_____
_____
_____
_____
_____
_____
_____
_____
_____
_____
_____
_____
_____
_____
_____
_____
_____
_____
_____

MY JOURNAL

_____
_____
_____
_____
_____
_____
_____
_____
_____
_____
_____
_____
_____
_____
_____
_____
_____
_____
_____
_____
_____
_____
_____
_____
_____
_____
_____
_____
_____
_____

MY JOURNAL

MY JOURNAL

_____

_____

_____

_____

_____

_____

_____

_____

_____

_____

_____

_____

_____

_____

_____

_____

_____

_____

_____

_____

_____

_____

_____

_____

_____

_____